# CAMBRIDGE LIBRARY COLLECTION

*Books of enduring scholarly value*

## Cambridge

The city of Cambridge received its royal charter in 1201, having already been home to Britons, Romans and Anglo-Saxons for many centuries. Cambridge University was founded soon afterwards and celebrated its octocentenary in 2009. This series explores the history and influence of Cambridge as a centre of science, learning, and discovery, its contributions to national and global politics and culture, and its inevitable controversies and scandals.

## The Anglo-Saxon Cemetery at Girton College, Cambridge

The Anglo-Saxon cemetery at Girton College, Cambridge, was discovered in 1881, while ground was prepared for the construction of tennis courts. More of the cemetery was unearthed in 1886, when the foundations for the Tower Wing were being laid. The area was excavated under the supervision of Francis Jenkinson (1853–1923), and the urns and other material found on the site date it to roughly the fifth and sixth centuries CE. The graves contained domestic utensils – tweezers, needles, pots for food and cooking – and personal items, such as ivory combs and bronze brooches. Written by Girton alumnae Edith Hollingworth and Maureen O'Reilly, this detailed report of the excavations is based on notes left by Jenkinson, and was first published by Cambridge University Press in 1925. According to a contemporary reviewer, the work of Hollingworth and O'Reilly provides a 'duty to their College and a real service to archaeology'.

Cambridge University Press has long been a pioneer in the reissuing of out-of-print titles from its own backlist, producing digital reprints of books that are still sought after by scholars and students but could not be reprinted economically using traditional technology. The Cambridge Library Collection extends this activity to a wider range of books which are still of importance to researchers and professionals, either for the source material they contain, or as landmarks in the history of their academic discipline.

Drawing from the world-renowned collections in the Cambridge University Library, and guided by the advice of experts in each subject area, Cambridge University Press is using state-of-the-art scanning machines in its own Printing House to capture the content of each book selected for inclusion. The files are processed to give a consistently clear, crisp image, and the books finished to the high quality standard for which the Press is recognised around the world. The latest print-on-demand technology ensures that the books will remain available indefinitely, and that orders for single or multiple copies can quickly be supplied.

The Cambridge Library Collection brings back to life books of enduring scholarly value (including out-of-copyright works originally issued by other publishers) across a wide range of disciplines in the humanities and social sciences and in science and technology.

# The Anglo-Saxon Cemetery at Girton College, Cambridge

*A Report Based on the MS. Notes of the Excavations Made by the Late F.J.H. Jenkinson, M.A.*

E. J. HOLLINGWORTH
M. M. O'REILLY

CAMBRIDGE
UNIVERSITY PRESS

CAMBRIDGE UNIVERSITY PRESS

Cambridge, New York, Melbourne, Madrid, Cape Town,
Singapore, São Paolo, Delhi, Tokyo, Mexico City

Published in the United States of America by Cambridge University Press, New York

www.cambridge.org
Information on this title: www.cambridge.org/9781108045049

© in this compilation Cambridge University Press 2012

This edition first published 1925
This digitally printed version 2012

ISBN 978-1-108-04504-9 Paperback

# THE ANGLO-SAXON CEMETERY

### AT

# GIRTON COLLEGE, CAMBRIDGE

# CAMBRIDGE
### UNIVERSITY PRESS
LONDON : Fetter Lane

NEW YORK
The Macmillan Co.

BOMBAY, CALCUTTA and
MADRAS
Macmillan and Co., Ltd.

TORONTO
The Macmillan Co. of
Canada, Ltd.

TOKYO
Maruzen-Kabushiki-Kaisha

# THE ANGLO-SAXON CEMETERY

AT

# GIRTON COLLEGE, CAMBRIDGE

A Report based on the MS. notes of the excavations made by the late F. J. H. Jenkinson, M.A.

BY

## E. J. HOLLINGWORTH

AND

## M. M. O'REILLY

CAMBRIDGE
AT THE UNIVERSITY PRESS
1925

# NOTE

THE antiquities discussed in the following pages are, with a very few exceptions, in the Cambridge University Museum of Archaeology and of Ethnology; some were presented at the time of the excavations; the rest were preserved at Girton College until 1924, when the Council of the College deposited them in the Museum as a Loan.

We wish to take this opportunity of expressing our thanks first to Miss B. S. Phillpotts, who whilst Mistress of Girton, suggested that this Report should be made, for her constant help and encouragement; and secondly to Dr Cyril Fox for his unfailing kindness in supervising our work.

We are indebted to Mr L. C. G. Clarke, Curator of the University Museum of Archaeology and of Ethnology, for his kindness in allowing us access to the objects preserved in the Museum.

Finally, we must make grateful acknowledgment to the Council of Girton College for their generous grant towards the publication of this Report. Our thanks are also due to the Syndics of the University Press for undertaking the publication of the work.

The photographs were taken by Mr W. Tams of Cambridge.

E. J. H.
M. M. O'R.

*October* 1925.

# CONTENTS

# ILLUSTRATIONS

# THE ANGLO-SAXON CEMETERY
# AT GIRTON COLLEGE

**Position.** The cemetery, which is situated on a bed of old river gravel, lies a few yards north of the Roman road from Cambridge to Godmanchester, at a distance of about two miles from Cambridge and about a mile south of the village of Girton.

**Discovery.** In 1881 the ground in front of Old Wing, then the whole of the newly-founded College at Girton, was being prepared for conversion into tennis courts, when some skeletons were discovered. The area of what is now the Emily Davies Court was then excavated under the supervision of the late Francis Jenkinson, M.A., of Trinity College, Cambridge, afterwards University Librarian. Mr Jenkinson kept a diary of the work as it proceeded, which he hoped to print, but unfortunately he never carried out this intention. His notes are exceedingly valuable because he recorded, not only the structure and contents of each grave, but also its exact position in relation to the others, and to the cremated burials. He went further and began to prepare a chart of the cemetery, which the directions left in his diary have enabled us to complete.

During the excavations about 150 cremation interments and 75–80 skeletons were discovered, all clearly referable to the Pagan Saxon period. Some Roman graves were brought to light and objects indicative of the existence of a Roman dwelling-house. A fragment of a Bronze Age cinerary urn was also found.

In 1886, when the foundations of the present Tower Wing of the College were being laid, some more urns were found. Baron von Hügel, Curator of the Cambridge Museum of Archaeology and Ethnology, thereupon obtained permission to excavate this further portion of the cemetery on the understanding, due no doubt to the conditions laid down in the contract with the builders, that the operations of the workmen were not to be delayed. With the help of Mr W. K. Foster, the Baron dug in advance of the workmen in a line with the trench already made by them, and to the lowest depth at which it was thought possible that the ground should ever have been disturbed. The work had to be carried on with the utmost expedition, the builders filling in the trench with cement on the heels of the excavators, and in the course of a fortnight's digging no further discoveries were made. They were about to give up the search, when the Baron struck with his spade into a skull a few inches below the depth at which they had been digging. At this depth the finds were abundant, but owing to the haste with which the excavators were compelled to proceed, they had barely time to remove the objects themselves and it was impossible to make any records of the position and association of their discoveries.

The following report from the *Proceedings of the Cambridge Antiquarian Society* is, therefore, the only existing account of Baron von Hügel's excavations:

"Baron von Hügel exhibited some antiquities found with skeletons at Girton in a field recently acquired by the college. The field extending along the high road (i.e. Roman road to Godmanchester) lies to the east of the present college buildings, and the skeletons were found within a stone's throw of the college. The collection included a pair of circular and 5 cross-shaped fibulae, strings of glass and amber beads, a bangle of Kimmeridge clay, a bronze girdlehanger (?), a pair of tweezers, a buckle, and two pairs of clasps. A large bone comb, spearheads and several iron knives were also found. Besides the skeletons 2 rough plain urns were exhumed, but it was impossible to get them entire out of the earth, and their contents yielded nothing worth preserving." (*Cambridge Antiquarian Society Comm.* Vol. VI, Rep. xlvi.) A list is given on p. 18 of the objects preserved in the Museum which were obtained during these excavations.

It is reported that Mr Jenkinson's workmen, who had previously been employed when the College was built in 1871, said that at that time they had found many similar urns. This suggests that the cemetery was larger than our plan indicates; it evidently extended northwards as well as eastwards.

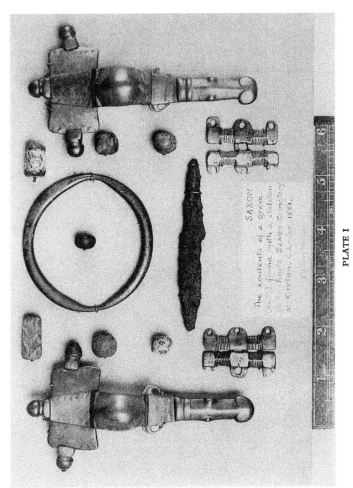

The contents of a grave
(found with a skeleton)
in the Anglo-Saxon Cemetery
at Girton, Cambs. 1881.

**PLATE I**

**TOMB-FURNITURE OF GRAVE 39**

## THE 1881 EXCAVATIONS: INHUMATION

The following tables show the contents of the graves and the objects associated with inhumation burials excavated in 1881. All the quotations are from Mr Jenkinson's MS notes, unless otherwise stated. (Objects mentioned in his notes which we have not been able to trace in the collection are printed in italics.)

### Table A

The following graves contained no objects at all:

| Grave | Position | Orientation | Stones, etc. |
|-------|----------|-------------|--------------|
| No. 16. 1 ft. 6 ins. deep. | "On back" | Head W. | "This body lay in the neighbourhood of many stones, but none of them seemed to belong to it." |
| No. 27. 2 ft. 3 ins. deep. | "Body lay straight. L. forearm across the body, forearm up to the chin." | Head SSW. | "No stones." |
| No. 36. 2 ft. deep. | "Person about 16 yrs old, lying on the back, hands on breast, head doubled down, feet sloping upwards." | Head SW. | — |
| No. 44. 2 ft. deep. | — | Head SW by W. | — |
| No. 50. Above 51. | — | Head S. | — |
| No. 59. | "Body had been laid on a neat platform of stones arranged on the gravel." | Head WNW. | — |
| No. 68. 1 ft. 6 ins. deep. | "Body lying flat; head and several bones gone." | Head NW. | — |

# Table B

## The following graves contained a knife only:

| Grave | Position | Orientation | Stones, etc. |
|---|---|---|---|
| No. 20. 3 ft. 3 ins. deep. | "A body much crushed and decomposed, on its back, head crushed down to R." | Head ESE by E. | Body lay "beneath at least a cart-load of very large stones." |
| No. 24. 1 ft. 3 ins. deep. | "Head missing except the jaws: legs from the knee also missing." | Head SE. | — |
| No. 42. 2 ft. deep. | "Head and bones fallen to R. L. forearm across body." | Head SE. | "Stones about grave small." |
| No. 48. 1 ft. 3 ins. deep. | "Bones lying in order." | Head S by E. | — |
| No. 49. | "Bones very well preserved." | Head SW by S. | — |
| No. 51. Below 50. | "Two interments occurred (50 and 51), one exactly above the other." | Head S. | — |
| No. 75. | "Body straight. L. hand up to breast, R. hand across belly." | Head NW. | "A few stones over the body, leaving the head free." |

## The following graves contained nails or scraps of iron only:

| Grave | Position | Orientation | Position of Nails, etc. |
|---|---|---|---|
| No. 30. 2 ft. deep. | "Body lying straight, arms by sides." | Head S by E. | "Some nails occurred by the head." |
| No. 32. 1 ft. 6 ins. deep. | "Bones apparently of a person in the prime of life." | Head SW¼S. | 1 large nail in pelvis. |
| No. 35. 2 ft. deep. | "Body lay on its back, the hands together on the R. lap....An old man, much afflicted with rheumatoid arthritis." | Head S by W. | 1 nail at feet. |
| No. 38. | Child "about 8 yrs old." | Head ENE. | "An unintelligible scrap of iron occurred behind the body." |

## Table C

The following graves contained pottery only, or pottery and a few nails or scraps of iron:

| Grave | A.S. vessels | Roman vessels | Nails, etc. |
|---|---|---|---|
| No. 12. Head NW. | "Urn[1] with 12 bosses—empty" (v. Pl. VI, 1). | — | — |
| No. 29. Head S. 3 ft. deep. "R. forearm vertical." | — | "*Vase of common reddishwhitespeckled 'biscuit ware,' i.e. Roman.*" | — |
| No. 34. Feet NNE. "Head and 1st 3 vertebrae lay between feet." | — | Castor ware beaker with trellis pattern in slip (v. Pl. VI, 8). | 1 nail at feet, 1 at R. side. |
| No. 37. Head NE½E. "Child of 14 yrs old. Legs sloped upwards." | Near face a "basin, broken." | — | — |
| No. 43. Head NW by W. "A large and strong man." | A vessel, "perhaps a food-vessel, was entangled among the R. clavicle and and rib bones." | — | — |
| No. 52. Head S. A child. | "Small cup, unbroken, behind head." | — | — |
| No. 57. Head SE¼E. "Stones on this grave very large, 23 in number." | "A very delicate vase of Saxon fabric, in a coarse cup stood outside the R. arm." | — | — |

[1] Mr Jenkinson used the term "urn" indiscriminately for any type of pottery vessel; he was careful to state, however, whether or no a vessel contained bones, so that it is possible to distinguish between a cinerary urn and a decorated vessel of so-called cinerary urn type used as accessory vessel, as in this grave.

(N.B.) Frequent references are made in the following tables to plates in the following books:

G. Baldwin Brown, *Saxon Art and Industry*, vols. 3 and 4, cited as *Brown*.

C. Fox, *Archaeology of the Cambridge Region*, cited as *Fox*.

Table D

Graves with some associated objects:

| Grave | Position of skeleton | Fibulae | Buckles | Knives | Toilet implements | Pottery | Miscellaneous | Remarks |
|---|---|---|---|---|---|---|---|---|
| No. 2. | Depth 2½ ft. Head to NW. | 1 small cruciform (Pl.IV,3). 1 Roman (Pl. IV, 3). | — | — | — | — | — | — |
| No. 3. | Depth 3 ft. Head NW. "Legs bent." | — | — | 1 (as Brown, Pl. XXVIII, 18). | 1 pr bronze tweezers. | Over head "plain urn," i.e. food-vessel. | — | Grave covered with "large mass of rect-angular stones." "One cylindrical." |
| No. 4. | Depth 3 ft. Head SSW. | — | — | 1 | 1 pr minute tweezers. Small bronze toothpick. | At left of heel "small plain urn," i.e. food-vessel. | — | — |
| No. 6. | Depth 2 ft. Head W by N. "Body on left side." | — | 1 large iron buckle (as Brown, Pl. LXX, 2). | 1 | — | Before face "fragments of pot." | — | — |
| No. 8. | Depth 2½ ft. Head SSW. | — | — | — | — | — | — | — |
| No. 8 a. A child's. | Head to SW. | — | — | — | — | — | 1 spearhead as Brown, Pl. XXXII. | — |
| No. 9. | Depth 3 ft. Head to SSW. | — | — | — | 1 pr bronze tweezers. | Over body "small urn" (i.e. accessory vessel), empty. | Iron axehead (Pl. IV, 4), Roman brick embedded in mortar. | "Stones round W side and halfway down E side." |

| | | | | | | | | |
|---|---|---|---|---|---|---|---|---|
| No. 13. | Depth 2 ft. 3 ins. "Straight." Head SSW. "Skeleton much decomposed." | 2 cruciform fibulae. 1 small-long (as Brown, Pl. XLII, 1). | — | — | — | — | — | "A stone by the R. shoulder and another under the femur." |
| No. 17. | Depth 2½ ft. Head to W. | — | — | — | — | — | "Flat jet (?) bead about 1 in. in diameter." | "The workmen in levelling the earth found a bronze bell" (apparently unconnected with grave). |
| No. 18. | Depth 2½ ft. "Head lying against right femur of 17." | — | 1 iron. | 1 (small) (as Brown, Pl. XXVIII, 14). | — | By head "fragment of urn." | — | — |
| No. 21. An old woman. | Depth 1 ft. 10 ins. Head ESE. "Doubled up." | — | — | 1 as above. | — | — | Beads. | — |
| No. 23, Male skeleton. | Depth 18 ins. Head S. "Lower jaw by L. elbow." | — | — | 1 (small) as above. | — | — | "Rolled piece of bronze" about 1½ ins. long. | — |
| No. 26. | Depth 3 ft. Head to ESE. "Straight." "Very stout." | — | — | — | — | — | At right shoulder spearhead 11½ ins. long. | — |
| No. 28. | Depth 15 ins. Head to SSW. "Straight." | — | "2 scraps of flat bronze, 1 at R. shoulder, 1 at R. hip, with 1 or 2 holes in them"—buckles? | — | — | "Durobrivian vase" (v. Pl. VI, 7). Pieces of Roman pottery including Samian ware. | Charcoal. Burnt bone. A few nails. | — |
| No. 31. | Depth 2½ ft. Head NW. Straight. | — | 1 iron. | 1 | Bone pin—moulded head, pierced. | — | On R. shoulder spearhead 10¾ ins. long. | — |
| No. 41. | Depth 2 ft. 2 ins. Head W½S. On R. side. | — | — | — | — | — | — | — |

Table D (continued)

| Grave | Position of skeleton | Fibulae | Buckles | Knives | Toilet implements | Pottery | Miscellaneous | Remarks |
|---|---|---|---|---|---|---|---|---|
| No. 46. | Depth 1 ft. 6 ins. Head SW. | — | — | — | — | — | "In pelvis *iron* *ring*," | — |
| No. 47. | Depth 2 ft. 3 ins. Head SW⅓S. | — | — | — | — | — | By R. shoulder "bronze rim of pail." | — |
| No. 55. | Head E. | 1 large cruciform. | — | — | — | — | Bead, 1 amber. | — |
| No. 58. Child. | Head W by S. | — | — | — | — | — | Miniature spear by R. shoulder. | — |
| No. 69. | Depth 1½ ft. Head S by E. | — | At L. hip small bronze buckle. Iron pin and hinge remaining. | — | 1 pr tweezers above R. hip. | — | — | — |
| No. 70. | Head NNE. | — | 1 iron. | 1 | — | — | — | — |
| No. 72. | Depth 1 ft. 8 ins. Head NE by E½E. | — | — | 1 | — | — | "Bronze binding & clamp like pieces of bronze." | — |
| No. 74. | Head SSW. | — | — | — | Comb, pyramidal back (Pl. V, 2). | — | Bone spindle whorl. | Roman melon bead. |

Table E

Graves with a fairly rich deposit:

| Grave | Position | Fibulae | Beads and rings | Belt fittings, buckles and clasps | Toilet implements | Knives | Miscellaneous | Pottery | Remarks |
|---|---|---|---|---|---|---|---|---|---|
| No. 5. Male. | 4 ft. deep. "On back. Head WNW. Legs bent." | — | 1 bronze ring. | — | 1 pr bronze tweezers on ring with ear-pick. | 1 (as Brown, Pl. XXVIII, 14). | 1 bronze bound wooden situla (v. Pl. VI, 2). | — | |
| No. 11. 2 skeletons. | 1 skeleton lay full-length; the "other at left shoulder of 1st, with R. arm over L. arm of 1st." | 1 small-long (as Brown, Pl. XLII, 1). | 21 beads. | — | Iron pin. | 1 (as Brown, Pl. XXVIII, 14). | — | — | Jenkinson's MS does not mention stones, but has sketch of grave showing a large no. in much dis-order round it. |
| No. 15. Child. | 1 ft. 6 ins. deep. Head E. | — | 1 "vinous glass bead, 1 spiral bronze ring (finger)." | 1 rectangular bronze plate, probably belt plate (cf. B.M.G. p. 44). | — | — | — | — | Belt plate has small S-shaped ornament in centre. |
| No. 19. Male. | 2 ft. 9 ins. deep. Head SSW by S. "On back, very straight. Head turned on R. side." | — | 30 beads: 9 am-ber, 2 inlaid, 18 minute plain glass, 1 minute blown glass (as Brown, Pl. CIV, 1 a, c, and 2 and Pl. CVI, 5). | 2 iron buckles (as Brown, Pl. LXX, 2). | — | 1 (as Brown, Pl. XXVIII, 14). | *Bronze triangle.* Scrap of iron. | — | Scrap of iron lay behind head. Beads "mostly under R. cheek." Buckles at waist and shoulder blade. |
| No. 40. | 2 ft. 6 ins. deep. SE by S. "Legs bent." | 2 small-long, 1 sq.-headed, 1 trefoil-headed (as Fox, Pl. XXXIV, 3 and 4). | 1 small bronze ring. Blue glass beads and 2 amber. | 1 bronze buckle "with plain bronze plate." | — | — | *"Thin bronze triangle with dints on it and a hole broken away."* | — | Bronze triangle was "resting against the fib-ula." |
| No. 56. "Whether 2 interments un-certain." Male. | Head NW. "Hardly any bones remain-ed." | — | — | 1 iron buckle (as Brown, Pl. LXX, 2). | — | — | 1 bronze-hoop-ed wooden sit-ula (cf. Pl. VI, 2). "Some Roman bricks embedded in cement." 1 bronze basin. | — | Basin lay over face. "When this was lifted a layer of bracken fern, on which it had been laid, was clearly visible, some of the fronds having been pre-served by the superincumbent metal" (C. A. S. Rep. XLI). |

## Table F

Graves with a rich deposit:

| Grave | Position | Fibulae | Clasps, buckles, etc. | Other ornaments | Toilet implements | Knives | Miscellaneous | Accessory vessels | Remarks |
|---|---|---|---|---|---|---|---|---|---|
| No. 7. | Depth 4 ft. | 2 cruciform, detachable side knobs. | 1 pr clasps (as Gr. 39, Pl. I). | *Beads* | — | — | Bronze ring flat in section, 4 in. in diameter | — | — |
| ["3 yds. north-west of Gr. 7, small pieces of oolite were numerous...no grave could be found...but presently a ring-brooch turned up, flat, one-sided, with shallow ornamentation" (Quoit brooch, v. Pl. IV, 2 c).] | | | | | | | | | |
| No. 10. | Depth 2 ft. 2 ins. Head SSW. | — | Set of bronze belt-fittings (v. Fox, Pl. XXXV, 1). | — | 1 pr iron tweezers. | — | — | — | "Boundary of stones" round this grave. |
| No. 25. | Depth 2 ft. 3 ins. Head WNW. | 2 small-long (as Fox, Pl. XXXIV, 3 and 4). | — | Beads: 7 inlaid vitreous paste, 10 blue glass, 6 vitreous paste. Bronze pin with coiled head. | Bronze earpick with spiral shaft, hung on ring. | — | Roman 3rd brass coin pierced, illegible. | — | Skeleton crouching, "Face downwards into a pot," much broken. |
| No. 33. | Depth 2 ft. in. Head SSW. | 3 fibulae: (1) cruciform, cast side knobs, very small, (2) cruciform, detachable side knobs, (3) small-long (as Brown, Pl. XLII, 1, 4). | — | Beads: 9 amber, 1 multi-coloured vitreous paste, 1 blue glass. Bronze ring 1 in. in diameter under beads. | — | — | Fragments of iron scattered about grave. | — | N.B. Peculiarity of fibulae. Smaller fibula has undeveloped horse's head and cast side knobs. Larger has well developed horse's head and detachable side knobs. |
| No. 39 (v. Pl. I). | Depth 2 ft. Head NNE. "Only skull, leg and arm bones remained." | 1 pair cruciform. | 1 pair wrist-clasps. | 18 beads. | — | 1 | Bronze ring, 2¼ ins. in diam. | — | Grave covered by stones. |
| No. 45. | Head NW. | 1 pair trefoil-headed small-long. | 1 pair wrist-clasps (as Gr. 39, Pl. I). | Beads: 21 vitreous paste, 3 multicoloured vitreous paste. | — | 1 | Roman 3rd brass coin, pierced, illegible. | — | — |

| | | | | | | | | | |
|---|---|---|---|---|---|---|---|---|---|
| No. 54. | "A few scattered bones only." | 1 pr trefoil-headed small-long. | 1 pr wrist-clasps (as Gr. 39, Pl. I). | 1 bronze finger ring. 2 bronze rings with slip knots, 3 beads on each. 20 beads, blue glass, 1 amber. | — | — | Roman 3rd brass coin, pierced, illegible. | — | "Some of the cloth preserved by verdigris to the fibula." |
| No. 71 (v. Pl. II). | Depth 2 ft. Head NNE. "Body on R. side." | 1 trefoil-headed, small-long. 1 pr sq.-headed, small-long. | 1 pr clasps. | 70 beads (3 inlaid, 37 blue glass, 30 self-coloured. 1 knob of cruciform fibula, pierced). | 1 pr bronze tweezers. | 1 | "Large iron ring behind hips." Bone spindle whorl. | 2 vessels, "1 delicate, the other coarser" (v. Pl. VI, 3). Fragments of third vessel. | The 2 complete vessels were behind the heels, the fragments on the instep. |

The following groups of objects are in the Cambridge Museum, labelled "Girton College, 1881"; they are not, however, described in Jenkinson's notes, as we have them, and must have come from graves the record of which is lost.

| | | | | | | | | | |
|---|---|---|---|---|---|---|---|---|---|
| Group I (v. Fox, Pl. XXVII, 2). | — | 1 pr disc. 1 large cruciform. | 1 pr wrist-clasps (1 piece odd). | 1 girdle-hanger. | — | — | 1 pr bronze objects, resembling broken halves of a pr. of tweezers, but each having a complete loop for suspension, containing iron. | — | — |
| Group II. | — | 1 pr applied (foundations only remain). | 1 pr wrist-clasps, broken. 1 minute bronze buckle. | Ivory, ring 4 ins. in diam. 1 pair girdle-hangers, suspended from small iron ring which is attached to larger iron ring. | — | — | — | — | — |

Group III. 2 quoit brooches, not a pair. One mended with a piece of metal riveted on.
Group IV. 1 pr sq.-headed small-long fibulae, as Fox, Pl. XXX, 5.
Group V. 1 pr sq.-headed small-long fibulae, as Fox, Pl. XXX, 5.
Group VI. Trefoil-headed small-long fibula.

The following objects had been preserved at Girton College until the removal of all the objects to the Cambridge Museum; they must therefore belong to the 1881 group, although they are not mentioned in Jenkinson's notes, nor do we know what graves they come from:

1 bone comb-case (Pl. V, 1).

1 large cruciform fibula with cast side-knobs.

Half a pair of wrist-clasps.

The following objects have been sent to the Museum by Mr Jenkinson's executors; they are labelled "Girton College" and must belong to the 1881 group:

(1) In one box were portions of 2 skulls and jaw-bones with the following objects:

   1 spearhead, 15 ins. long.   1 small lancehead, 5·3 inches long.

   2 umbos, iron, of the form usually found in this district (v. Fox, Pl. XXXVI).

   1 knife, 7 ins. long.

   Fragments of Roman pottery, of the type usually found on this site; a fragment of a glazed tile.

(2) A group dated "March 26" including:

   1 stout bronze ring, 1 in. in diameter.

   1 knife, 4 ins. long.

   1 pr bronze tweezers.

   A stick of cut bone broadening out into blade form at one end.

   A fragment of iron.

(3) A group including:

   1 knife, 3½ ins. long.

   Fragments of 2 or more combs.

   1 scrap of bronze.

   2 Roman coins, 1 illegible, the other of Constantine—both pierced for suspension.

(4) 1 bronze spearhead, 8 ins. long.

(5) Fragments of a bronze penannular fibula.

(6) 1 glass bead.

(7) 1 fine pair of bronze tweezers (Pl. IV, 1 a).

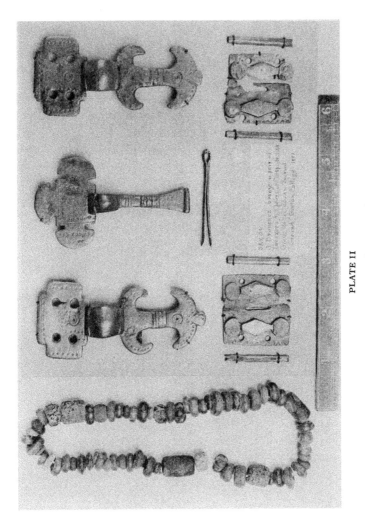

**PLATE II**

TOMB-FURNITURE OF GRAVE 71

## ARRANGEMENT OF INHUMATION BURIALS

A glance at the accompanying plan will show that there was little attempt at systematic arrangement in this cemetery. The distribution of graves and urns, as well as the associated tomb furniture, indicates that inhumation and cremation were practised here contemporaneously throughout the whole Pagan Saxon period. No special quarter was given over to either rite. A thick belt of urns runs at right angles to the Roman road and the majority of the inhumation graves are scattered round this central zone in more or less congested groups, but inhumation graves are frequent in the urn-belt and many urns occur among the outlying inhumation graves.

No particular area was allotted to the wealthy. In the north-easternmost group, for instance, Grs. 39 and 71, two of the richest in the cemetery, are surrounded by Grs. 37, 73, 69, 70 and 41, five of the poorest.

We cannot point to any one part of the cemetery as having been occupied earlier than any other part. In the group mentioned above Gr. 34 is apparently that of one of the earliest settlers, while Gr. 71 may be dated in the early years of VI. In another area Gr. 2 is early, Gr. 10 is undoubtedly late. This shows that interments were not made regularly, one quarter having been exhausted before another was entered, but that they were made sporadically in various quarters at the same time. It is unlikely, judging from this confusion, that any permanent memorials, such as tombstones or mounds, marked the site of each grave, and it is very doubtful whether even wood was used for the purpose.

The bodies were buried in graves dug out of the gravel at depths varying from 4 ft. (Nos. 5 and 7) to 1 ft. 3 ins. (Nos. 24 and 48), the average depth being 2 ft. 3 ins. One grave only was "hollowed out of the gault" (No. 20); at this point, evidently, the overlying gravel deposit was thin.

Nails were found in several graves, but in one only were they placed so as to suggest a coffin (No. 28).

In 17 graves some attempt had been made to protect the body by placing stones round it or above it. Stones formed the boundaries of Nos. 9, 10 and 12. The entire skeleton in Nos. 3, 8, 20 and 57 was covered by a mass of large stones. Stones had been placed over the head in Nos. 22 and 26, and in 3 more graves, Nos. 41, 56 and 75, the body was covered but the head was free. Gr. 40 was covered with pieces of oolite "mostly small." The structure of Gr. 59 was unusual, the body having been "laid on a neat platform of stones."

**Orientation.** The following list shows the directions in which the heads of the skeletons pointed:

| | | | | |
|---|---|---|---|---|
| NNE | ... | 3 | S by W... | 1 |
| NE | ... | 1 | SSW ... | 10 |
| NE by E | | 1 | SSW by S | 1 |
| ENE | ... | 1 | SW by S | 1 |
| E | ... | 1 | SW ... | 4 |
| ESE | ... | 2 | SW by W | 2 |
| ESE by S | | 2 | WSW ... | 4 |
| SE | ... | 3 | W by S... | 1 |
| S by E | ... | 3 | W ... | 4 |
| S | ... | 5 | W by N | 2 |
| | | 22 | WNW ... | 3 |
| | | | NW by W | 3 |
| | | | NW ... | 7 |
| | | | | 43 |

The 10 skeletons with head to SSW are not buried in contiguous graves, but are scattered over the whole area of the cemetery; the same is true of the 4 pointing W. It is obvious, therefore, that in no quarter was there any attempt at uniformity of orientation. The confusion prevalent here is paralleled most closely at Kempston, Beds., where the bodies were "deposited at all angles with one another and directed to almost every point of the compass" (Brown, p. 166).

**Disposal.** The positions of 42 of the skeletons are noted by Mr Jenkinson.

| | | | | |
|---|---|---|---|---|
| "On back. Straight" | ... | ... | | 25 |
| Legs flexed | ... | ... | ... | 14 |
| On side | ... | ... | ... | 3 |

**Exceptional Burials.** The following passages from the MS describe some unusual burials.

Gr. 25. "The body of a girl of about 14 lay in a narrow compass. The face was downwards into an urn[1] which had apparently been a food-vessel."

[1] Mr Jenkinson does not confine his use of the term "urn" to sepulchral vessels associated with cremation interments.

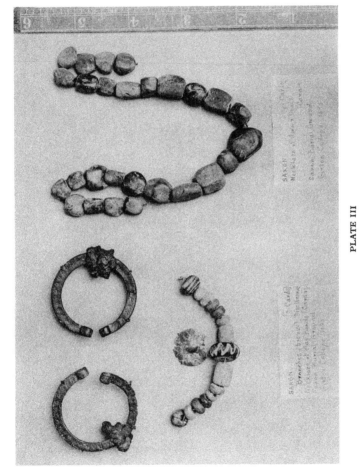

**PLATE III**

GROUP C (1886 EXCAVATIONS)

Gr. 29. "Body straight, head thrown back; right forearm vertical (in fact first bones found)."

Two double interments were found.

Gr. 11. "On the SE side lay a skeleton at full length; a knife by the right arm, legs crossed at ankles. On its left shoulder another with right arm exactly over the other's left: body straight, legs closely doubled, knees above the other's. With this second skeleton occurred a single fibula on the left clavicle, near which were 21 beads....Near them what may be an iron pin. Bones of the two equal: femur 17½: tibia 14½: No. 1 a trifle stouter."

Grs. 17 and 18. "There was a fragment of urn by the head, a stone by the right shoulder and another by the femur (behind the head of the second skeleton)....The bones, though not long (femur hardly 18 ins.) suggested great strength, while the teeth were in perfect condition....Against the right femur of the last skeleton, and inside it, was the head of another, lying straight. ...Femur 19 ins. Face upwards."

The most remarkable interment of all was that in Gr. 34. "11 ft. from E, 44 ft. from G, at 2 ft. deep occurred a Durobrivian vase; rather globular, 5 ins. high....This vase was proved to be at the left shoulder of a skeleton duly laid out: feet to NNE. The head and three first vertebrae lay between the feet. Length without head 4 ft. 8. Femur 17¼ ins. Tibia 14 ins. A few stones on the left side. A nail at the right side, another at feet."

Prof. Baldwin Brown mentions a similar interment at White Horse Hill, Berks. (vol. III, p. 154).

It is impossible not to think in this connection of such incidents in the Icelandic Sagas as the laying of the ghost of Kar the Old. "Grettir then drew his sword Jokulsnaut, and cut off the head of the howe-dweller and laid it between his thighs" (*Grettissaga*, ch. 18). The same procedure was adopted after Glam had been vanquished. "Grettir drew his short sword, cut off Glam's head and laid it between his thighs" (*Ibid.* ch. 35).

**Children's Graves.** Out of a total of 75 graves, 10 were those of children (Nos. 6, 6 a, 23 a, 25, 36, 37, 38, 48, 52, 58).

Three more were lying in the Roman rubbish pit. No differences can be detected between the manner of their burial and that of the adults (*v.* Brown, p. 189 ff.). The system of orientation adopted for children was not uniform. There was nothing remarkable about the disposal of any of them except the 14-year old girl in Gr. 25. It may be noted that in two cases, Grs. 36 and 37, "the legs sloped upwards." This may possibly be the effect of some peculiarity of the ground, and unintentional. As regards Tomb Furniture the same variety exists as among the older people. One grave (No. 25) was richly furnished. Four had no objects. The remaining 5 graves each contained 1 object.

**Accessory Vessels.** These were chiefly of pottery in this cemetery, but occasionally vessels of wood or of metal were used.

(1) *Pottery.* 14 vessels were found—9 graves contained 1 each; 1 grave had 2 and another 3 vessels. These are mostly small cup-shaped or bowl-shaped vessels, hand-made, ranging in colour from buff to dark-brown (e.g. Pl. VI, 4). Gr. 12, however, contained a small vessel of cinerary urn type, decorated with 10 bosses and incised lines (Pl. VI, 1).

Four other graves (Nos. 7, 14, 17 and 33) are said by Jenkinson to have contained pottery vessels, but we have not been able to identify them, and his notes do not make it clear whether they were associated with the inhumation interments or were merely cinerary urns accidentally encroaching on the graves.

As a rule accessory vessels were placed near the head of the skeleton. In Gr. 57, however, 2 vessels were found, both near the arm; and in Gr. 71 "behind the heels were 2 vessels, 1 rather delicate" (Pl. VI, 3), "the other coarser; ... in front of the left instep was another vessel, more open, part lost."

(2) *Wood.* Grs. 5 and 56 contained accessory vessels of wood (*v.* Pl. VI, 2). These are small situlae, about 5 ins. high bound with circular bands and 4 uprights of bronze; 2 curved strips of bronze in the shape of animal heads are riveted to the sides and evidently formed part of the handle, the rest of which is missing. In both graves the situla lay by the head of the skeleton, with which was associated a second vessel—a pottery vessel in Gr. 5 and a bronze basin in Gr. 56.

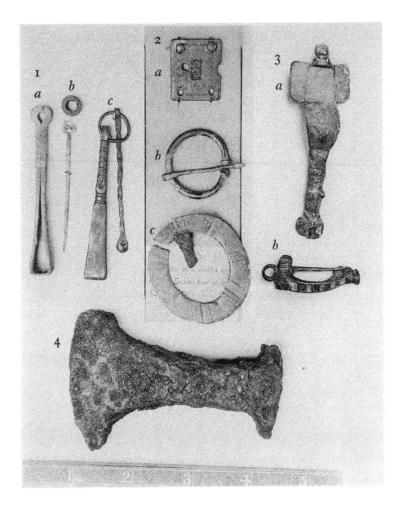

### PLATE IV

1, TOILET IMPLEMENTS AND PIN      2 *a*, BELT PLATE, GRAVE 8
2 *b*, FIBULA FROM URN     2 *c*, ANNULAR FIBULA     3, ASSOCIATED
FIBULAE, GRAVE 2          4, AXE-HEAD, GRAVE 9

(3) *Basins or cooking-pots.* Grs. 37 and 56 contained bronze basins or cooking-pots. That in Gr. 37 was placed "near the face." This vessel was much broken, and only a few scraps of bronze and part of the rim remain; the fragment of rim has a series of small bosses beaten up from underneath. In Gr. 56 the basin was "crushed against the side of the grave." "When this basin was lifted, a layer of bracken fern on which it had been laid was clearly visible, some of the fronds having been preserved by the superincumbent metal" (*C.A.S. Rep.* XLI). This basin has a "flat rim and ears for handles" (cf. Brown, Pl. CXVII, 3 and p. 472).

(4) *Roman Pottery.* Fragments of Roman pottery were frequently found in or near the Anglo-Saxon graves (e.g. Grs. 29 and 33) but these fragments appear to have been scattered in the soil covering the grave, and to have no connection with the interment.

Two graves, however, Nos. 28 and 34, contained each a beaker of Castor ware, placed, in both graves, by the head of the skeleton. These beakers are of 4th century type; neither grave contains any associated object except a few nails and scraps of bronze. These graves may therefore belong to the Roman or to the Anglo-Saxon period. Since the site was used for Roman cremation burials it is quite likely that it should have been used for inhumations also. On the other hand, there is nothing in the arrangement of the graves—e.g. a stone cist or lead coffin—that might suggest that they are Roman; and although it is unusual for Roman pottery to be placed deliberately in an Anglo-Saxon grave, it is not impossible here, since the vessels are of so late a date.

Gr. 34 contains the remarkable burial described above, in which the head of the skeleton was cut off and laid between the legs. This does not help one to a solution of the problem of whether these are Roman or Saxon graves. The custom was a purely Teutonic one, but although this example of it proves that the people who practised it here were Teutonic, it does not prove that the person on whom they practised it was Teutonic also; the person who caused the disturbance was in fact as likely, in the circumstances, to have been a Romanised Briton as a Saxon or Angle.

Jenkinson evidently supposed these two graves to be Roman, as he painted them in red in his plan of the cemetery; the two Roman cremation burials are painted in red also, while all the other burials are in black.

Before going on to discuss the objects, it will be convenient to give a list of the objects from the 1886 excavations preserved in the Museum:

### Objects from the 1886 Excavations

Group A    1 pr penannular brooches, with coiled ends.
(v. Pl. III). Amber beads.
           1 small silver pendant, with border of Y-shaped units.
Group B.    2 small-long fibulae.
           1 pr tweezers (bronze).
           1 small bronze buckle.
           Beads, blue and yellow clear glass, cylindrical.
           1 large black bead.
Group C.    2 sq.-headed small-long fibulae (v. Fox, Pl. XXX, 5).
           10 beads—7 blown-glass, 3 small inlaid.
Group D.    1 bangle of Kimmeridge shale.
           5 prs of bronze tweezers and 2 shield-bosses, broken, are also preserved in the Museum. They are not mentioned in either account and are not dated.

### OBJECTS OF SPECIAL INTEREST ASSOCIATED WITH BURIALS

These may be divided into two classes, objects of intrinsic interest of rare design or type, and group finds which give chronological data.

### 1. Objects of intrinsic interest

The range of types in this cemetery is somewhat limited and the objects themselves, on the whole, are plain and unambitious in workmanship. Those most commonly found, such as fibulae and buckles, are usually small and plain. The following, however, are noteworthy.

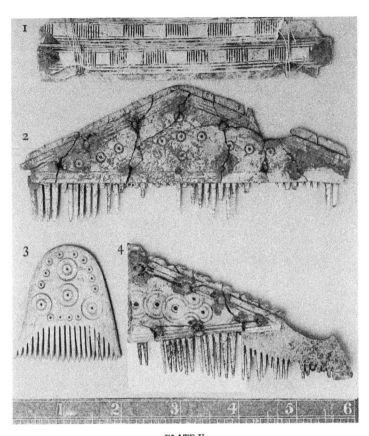

PLATE V

COMBS AND COMB-CASE

A. Dress Ornaments.

   (1) Gilt belt-fittings. Gr. 10.

   (2) A child's belt-plate. Gr. 8.

   (3) Cruciform fibula (1886).

   (4) Pair of penannular brooches (1886).

   (5) Bangle of Kimmeridge shale (1886).

   (6) Shaft of girdle-hanger (1886).

   (7) Large bronze ring (1886).

B. Toilet Implements.

   (1) Comb case (1881).

   (2) Pins with coiled heads. 1886 and Gr. 25.

   (3) Pair of tweezers. Gr. 4.

   (4) Small bronze objects. Group I. 1881.

C. Drop-bladed axe. Gr. 9.

## A. Dress Ornaments

(1) *The complete set of belt-fittings* from Gr. 10 (Fox, Pl. XXXV) consists of a bronze buckle and 3 square plates, one of which is attached to the buckle. Each plate was fastened to the belt by means of 4 studs. The ornament, a four-leaf pattern or star design, is executed in relief, and the raised pattern is gilt. The workmanship is excellent and Fox says of the design that it is "characteristic of the best period of Anglian art in this district" (Fox, p. 248).

Similar ornament is to be seen on the disc from Lakenheath (Camb. Mus., Case 49); on the headplate of a cruciform fibula from St John's (Camb. Mus., Case 42) (and Fox, Pl. XXVII, 1); on the bead-clasps from Barrington (Camb. Mus., Case 41), and on a pair of wrist-clasps from Sleaford, Lincs., found in association with "a large cruciform fibula richly chased and gilt" (*Archaeologia*, vol. L, Pl. XXIII, 5).

Complete set of belt-fittings are very rare in other parts of England, but four more sets from this district are preserved, 2 from Barrington A, 1 from Haslingfield and 1 from St John's (*v.* Fox, footnote 1, p. 248).

(2) *Belt-plate from a child's grave* (Pl. IV, 2 a). The ornament

here shows classical influence. It consists of a border of con-
joined semicircles, with a small panel in the centre of the plate
containing an incised S-shaped design. The whole shows traces
of silver-plating (cf. *B.M.G.* Fig. 37).

(3) *A cruciform fibula*, one of the 1886 finds, is notable, as
the lower part of it, especially the horse's head, is more convex
than is usual in English types.

(4) *The penannular fibulae*, 2 of which are figured on Pl. IV,
are rare in this district; 4 were found associated with inhumation
burials; 3 of bronze and 1 of iron. The latter type is especially
rare.

(5) *A bangle of Kimmeridge shale* was found—this, again, is
an uncommon type in this district.

(6) *The shaft of a girdle-hanger* ornamented with a pattern
evidently derived from that on cruciform fibulae is interesting
both from the instance it provides of the appearance of similar
ornament on two widely different objects, and also because it
is exactly paralleled at Little Wilbraham (*v.* Fox, Pl. XXXIII, 5).

(7) *The stout bronze ring* from Gr. 39 (Pl. I), much worn on
its inner edge, may possibly have been used to attach small
articles to the belt, i.e. for the same purpose as the ordinary
"key" type of girdle-hanger.

## B. Toilet Implements

(1) The *comb-case* figured on Pl. V, 1, is a rare find. The
ornamentation consists simply of groups of incised parallel lines.
It may be compared with the comb case in the Brussels Mus.
figured by Brown on Pl. LXXXV, 2.

(2) The *bronze pins*, one with a single, another with a double
spiral coil at the head, suggest a La Tène origin; a third has a
knobbed head, cut in 14-plane surfaces.

(3) Among the numerous pairs of tweezers found, one pair
figured on Pl. IV, 1 c, is noteworthy for the excellence of its
workmanship, and as showing Roman influence in its design.

(4) In Group I (Fox, Pl. XXVII, 2) occur two small bronze
objects which might be taken for the broken halves of a pair of
tweezers but for the fact that there is incised ornament on what

PLATE VI

1, 2, 3, 4, ACCESSORY VESSELS, GRAVES 12, 56, 71, 37     5, 6, CINERARY URNS

7, 8, CASTOR WARE VASES, GRAVES 28, 34

would be the inner side of the tweezers, and that each part has a complete loop for suspension containing traces of iron, possibly from attachment to a girdle-hanger.

## C. Drop-bladed Axe

In Gr. 9 an axe-head of unusual type was found; the only other specimen found of this "drop-bladed" type discovered in this country was dredged out of the Thames, and is now in the Museum at Reading. Prof. Baldwin Brown shows that the type has affinities with W. France (Herpes) and with Hungary (v. Arts, p. 233 and Pl. XXX, 3).

### 2. Group Finds showing Association of Types

The more important group finds in this cemetery show so much uniformity of type that they throw little light on the dating of particular objects. They are useful, however, in suggesting the comparative dates of certain graves.

In the series of graves comprising Grs. 7, 33, 39, 45, 54 and 71, for instance, Grs. 7 and 39 have cruciform fibulae with detachable side-knobs in association with wrist-clasps of the type figured by Fox on his Plate XXXIV, 1 a; Gr. 33 has a similar fibula with clasps only very slightly different; Grs. 45 and 54 show similar clasps in association with trefoil-headed small-long fibulae of good design and workmanship; a similar fibula is found in Gr. 71. Beads of amber, of inlaid vitreous paste, of clear glass (mostly dark blue) and of opaque glass (mostly green and yellow) are found in all these graves. The other objects in these group finds are knives, buckles, and small rings of plain design such as are found throughout the period. Gr. 39, mentioned above, has also the bronze ring already discussed as, possibly, an early type of girdle-hanger.

This series of group finds is interesting because it indicates that the majority of rich graves in this cemetery were contemporaneous. Two other groups appear to be contemporaneous, Group I (1881, Fox, Pl. XXVII, 2) and Group II. The former contains a cruciform fibula with cast side-knobs and zoomorphic ornament; in association with this are a pair of disc fibulae, a girdle-hanger with moulded terminal, 103 amber beads, the bronze tweezer-like objects, described above, and a pair of wrist-clasps, flat, with a panel of "ladder" pattern incised in the centre. The "eye" part of one clasp is an odd piece; flat and ornamented with punch marks. Group II contains a pair of wrist-clasps of the same pattern as this odd piece, 41 amber beads, a pair of girdle-hangers, a pair of applied fibulae, a large ivory ring, a minute buckle and some scraps of bronze.

The question of the association of beads is an interesting one, but cannot be satisfactorily discussed, as we have not been able to identify the associations of all that were found. In the former series of finds (Grs. 7, 33, 39, 45, 54, 71), however, inlaid, dark blue glass, and small opaque glass beads seem to predominate.

| Gr. 7 | | | | |
|---|---|---|---|---|
| „ 33 | 9 amber | 1 inlaid | 1 blue glass | |
| „ 39 | — | 18 „ | — | |
| „ 45 | — | — | — | 21 small opaque |
| „ 54 | — | — | — | 6 „ „ |
| „ 71 | — | 3 inlaid | 37 blue glass | 3 „ „ |

While in Groups I and II, which the presence of the elaborate cruciform fibula shows to be later, the beads are practically all amber.

In a few graves Roman objects are associated with Anglo-Saxon objects. In Gr. 2 a small Roman fibula, arched, the front inlaid with squares of red and white enamel (Pl. IV, 3) was associated with a small cruciform fibula with side-knobs missing. Illegible third brass coins are found in Grs. 25, 45, 54. Gr. 74 contained a pyramid-backed comb of Roman type (v. Pl. V, 2), a melon bead and a bone spindle whorl of the normal Anglo-Saxon type.

## THE 1881 EXCAVATIONS: CREMATION

The following table gives a list of cremation burials with which one or more objects, other than pottery, were associated. In the majority of such burials there was an urn only. Mr Jenkinson's information does not, unfortunately, enable us, as a rule, to identify the urn and associated object.

Table showing contents of cinerary urns

| Urn | Fibulae | Toilet implements | Combs | Beads | Miscellaneous |
|---|---|---|---|---|---|
| Nr Gr. 4. | — | I pr minute tweezers (as Brown, Pl. LXXXVII, 5). | Fragments of comb. | — | Fragments of fused bronze. |
| E of Grs. 4 and 5. A group of seven. I Roman grey ware. | I small-long. | — | — | "Blue glass and coloured clay." | — |
| Nr Gr. 8. | — | — | ½ comb with curvilinear pattern (v. Pl. V, 4). | Fragments of fluted green glass. | — |
| "Row passing through Gr. 5." | 2 small-long. | — | Fragments of comb. | — | Fragments of fused bronze, "also a bracelet." |
| "Row passing, NNE through Gr. 5." | Cruciform fibula broken. | Pr bronze tweezers on ring. | Fragments of comb. | — | "Short; broad-bladed knife." |
| In Gr. 10 (broken by inhumation burial). | Fragments of saucer and sq.-headed fibulae (v. Fox, Pl. XXXV, 2). | — | — | — | — |
| "Several." Nr Gr. 17. | Fragments of side-knobs of cruciform fibula of late type (and urn, Pl. VII, 4). | — | Fragment of comb. ½ comb with plain back. | — | — |
| Nr Gr. 18. | — | I pr iron shears. | Comb. | — | I knife. |
| 2 nr Gr. 20. | — | I pr tweezers. | Fragments of comb. | — | "A great quantity of fused vitreous stuff." Bone needle. |
| 2 nr Gr. 23 (i) | Penannular fibula (v. Pl. IV, 2 b). | I pr tweezers, broken and mended with thread. | — | — | — |
| (ii) | 2 small-long. | — | — | — | I iron buckle, I pr girdle-hangers, I wrist-clasp. |

*Table showing contents of cinerary urns (continued)*

| Urn | Fibulae | Toilet implements | Combs | Beads | Miscellaneous |
|---|---|---|---|---|---|
| Group in Gr. 26. | — | 1 pr iron shears. | Bow-backed comb (v. Pl. V, 3; and urn, Pl. VIII, 2). | "*Fused beads.*" | Fragments of glass. (Grouped with comb in Camb. Mus., but not mentioned in MS are a pr of minute shears and bronze knife (?) possibly for em- broidery work.) |
| In Gr. 32. | — | — | — | — | Fused pieces of bronze |
| Group of 5 nr Gr. 35. | — | Pr tweezers, small with grooved head. | — | — | — |
| Group of 10 nr Gr. 57. | — | Pr of tweezers with ear-pick on ring. | | | |

A small gold chain threaded with beads (fused) is preserved in the Museum, but we do not know from what urn it came.

A fragment of thick greenish glass, roughly an inch square, preserved among the potsherds in the Museum, was found inset in the base of a pottery vessel. The MS notes give no account of this, although it was mentioned in the Report to the C.A.S. Apparently this window-urn was broken either in course of excavation or immediately after, as no trace of it apart from the glass fragment has ever been found.

PLATE VII

CINERARY URNS

## ARRANGEMENT OF CREMATION BURIALS

Cremation burials are almost invariably contained in urns, usually covered with one or more pieces of stone. The plan shows that urns were arranged both in parallel rows and in confused groups.

Cinerary urns were frequently found very close to inhumation burials. Sometimes they were apparently broken when the inhumation interment was made, e.g. Gr. 10; sometimes they were put in the ground later and encroached on an earlier inhumation burial, e.g. Gr. 4, where an "urn containing bones" was found "directly over the head"; Gr. 32, where a "Saxon urn with bones" was found "over the knees," and a "broken Roman urn also containing bones" lay "clear of the left shoulder"; and Gr. 43, where a small urn in fragments "lay outside the left elbow and still contained bones." From the wording of Mr Jenkinson's MS it would appear that he supposed these latter urns to have been placed deliberately in the inhumation graves; but such a practice is almost unknown in Anglo-Saxon cemeteries, and it is almost certain that the juxtaposition is purely accidental.

**Types.** Many different varieties of urn are represented. All are hand-made, and vary in colour from buff to dark brown.

(1) *Shape.* The majority are clumsily made, more or less rounded, and sometimes almost globular (Pl. VIII, 2). About 20 per cent. have a carinated shoulder, and narrow neck (Pl. VII, 1 and 3). Some are intermediate between these two types. An example is figured on Pl. VI, 5, of a smaller type with a carinated shoulder, well-modelled rim and moulded foot; about ½-dozen of these occur, their decoration varying as in the larger urns. Small cup-shaped vessels were also used occasionally as cinerary urns.

(2) *Decoration.* Many urns are undecorated. When decoration is present it consists sometimes of grooved lines only; sometimes of stamped patterns only; sometimes of bosses only; or sometimes of all together. The bosses are always outlined by incised lines, and the stamped patterns almost always arranged in horizontal zones or triangular areas enclosed by incised lines.

The following table shows the proportion in which the various forms of decoration were found.

| | Without decoration (Pl. VII, 4) | Bosses (Brown, Pl. CXXXIV) | Stamps (Pl. VII, 2) | Stamps and bosses (Pl. VII, 1) | Grooved lines (Brown,Pl. CXXXVI 2 n.) |
|---|---|---|---|---|---|
| Whole number | 26 % | 12 % | 31 % | 18 % | 13 % |
| Urns with carinated shoulder | 21 % | 23 % | 12 % | 35 % | 9 % |
| Urns without carinated shoulder | 26 % | 9 % | 40 % | 12½ % | 12½ % |

The following passage from the MS suggests that vessels of other material than pottery may have been used occasionally to contain ashes.

"The bronze hoop of a pail occurred rather shallow, 3 ft. NW of M (i.e. nr Gr. 42). A mass of burnt bones looked as if they had been contained in the pail and had bulged when it decayed, but no bronze rim or handle occurred, only this one hoop."

### OBJECTS ASSOCIATED WITH CREMATION BURIALS

More objects of interest are found associated with cremation burials here than is usual in Anglian cemeteries.

The objects most commonly found are tweezers and combs. The latter occur very frequently and many different types are represented (Pl. V). One comb (Pl. V, 4) is decorated with a curvilinear design; on most of the combs the ornament consists of incised lines and circle and dot patterns. Combs are almost invariably unburnt.

Eleven fibulae were found, mostly much fused and broken. One of these, the only one unburnt, is penannular (Pl. IV, 2 b). Five are small-long fibulae. Two are fragments of cruciform fibulae with side-wings and well-developed horse's head. Two interesting fragments were found in a broken urn in the corner of Gr. 10 (v. Fox, Pl. XXXV, 2). These are the remains of a saucer brooch with zoomorphic decoration, and of a square-

PLATE VIII

CINERARY URNS

headed brooch, the head-plate of which has both zoomorphic and geometric decoration, and the side-lobes (not figured) simple linear ornament. In the urn figured on Pl. VII, 4 were found the side-knobs of a cruciform fibula; these are very large and covered with elaborate zoomorphic decoration.

The following group of objects was found in a single urn: A pair of small-long brooches.

A pair of girdle-hangers.

Half a wrist-clasp of thin flat type with circular punch marks.

A small iron buckle with bronze attachments.

(N.B. Girdle-hangers and a pair of wrist-clasps of this type are found together in Group II, and 1 piece of a similar wrist-clasp in Group I, where it is associated with an elaborate cruciform fibula; they are evidently of rather late date—probably mid VI.)

Some fused fragments of glass were found, very thin, of a brownish colour. Glass vessels are rare in this district (v. Fox, p. 294).

Two Roman objects were found in urns; a bow-backed comb (Pl. V, 3) in the urn figured on Pl. VIII, 2; and a small gold chain threaded with small round beads, very much fused; this closely resembles a chain from Richborough in the Camb. Mus., Case 42.

## THE RANGE OF DATE OF THE CEMETERY

### (1) *Inhumation Burials*

The following objects suggest that inhumation was practised at a very early date in this cemetery:

(a) Roman objects:
A fibula (Gr. 2, Pl. IV).

A pyramid-backed comb (Gr. 74, Pl. V, 2).

Pottery, including Castor ware.

(b) Small cruciform fibula with detachable side-knobs. This fibula is of very early type and cannot well be dated later than the last third of V (Gr. 7).

The Roman objects, evidently loot of a not very valuable kind, indicate the presence of early settlers, as such delicate or insignificant objects can hardly have been preserved for more than two generations after the Conquest.

Evidence for the lower limit of date is given by the following objects:

(*a*) Cruciform fibula with cast side-knobs and zoomorphic decoration on side-wings and head-plate (Group I, Fox, Pl. XXVII, 2). This is probably rather later than mid VI (cf. Brown, Pl. XLIV and p. 268. Our fibula is one stage further in development than Brown's example).

(*b*) Gilt belt-plates and ornaments (Gr. 10, Fox, Pl. XXXV, 1, 2). A cremation of late VI (*v. infra*) was disturbed by this inhumation, which cannot therefore well be later than the end of VI.

Inhumation, therefore, was practised here from the last third of V until 600 or thereabouts. It may be noted that the majority of the richest graves, which have been shown to be roughly contemporaneous (*v.* p. 21) appear to belong to the end of V and the early years of VI, as the cruciform fibulae they contain are of the type usually assigned to such a period.

### (2) *Cremation Burials*

(*a*) *Types of Urns.* It does not seem possible at present to decide which types of urn described on p. 25 are early and which are late.

R. A. Smith states that "there is some evidence that in the migration period a bold profile and decoration in relief were gradually replaced by a plain contour and incised or stamped decoration; certain stages of the evolution can be traced in England during the cremation period" (*B.M.G.*, *Anglo-Saxon Period*, p. 21).

If this classification hold good, 44 per cent. of our urns belong to the later and 30 per cent. to the earlier period; the rest are undecorated. It seems most probable, however, that the development and fusion of various styles of decoration, etc., was already accomplished when the invaders reached England. O. Almgren (*Ältere Eisenzeit Götlands*, Pl. 32) shows that already in III, grooved lines representing earlier bosses, occurred on pottery; while the window urn from Kempston, Beds. (*V.C.H.* p. 183) held to be one of the earliest urns in England,

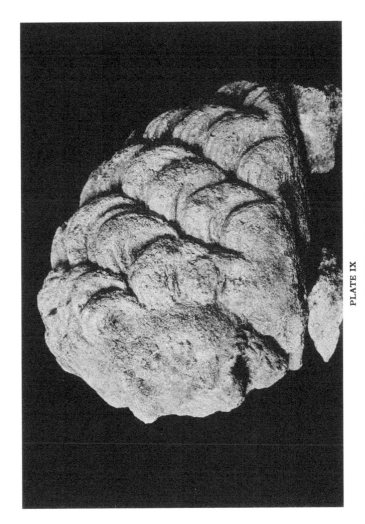

**PLATE IX**

SCULPTURED STONE, FROM RUBBISH-PIT

has the "bold profile," together with long bosses, or flutes, stamps, and incised lines.

Efforts to date the types of urn in this cemetery are rendered difficult by the fact that we have in most cases been unable to identify the urn in which a datable object was found. Two important objects, one early, the other late, a bow-backed comb and the knobs of a cruciform fibula, were found in undecorated urns (Pls. V, 3, VIII, 2, and VII, 4). It will be seen that the earlier urn is of the globose, the later of the shouldered type.

(b) *Contents of Urns.* The early date suggested by the window-urn (v. p. 24) is confirmed by the following objects:

Roman objects:

(1) Bow-backed comb.

(2) Fine gold chain threaded with blue beads.

The following objects suggest the lower limit of date:

(1) Pieces of side-knobs of cruciform fibula.

(2) Fragments of saucer and square-headed fibulae.

These objects were discussed on p. 26. They are so much fused that the detail of their design is difficult to follow. The saucer and square-headed fibulae, however, appear to have been well designed, and are not of degenerate type; they are probably not later than the end of VI.

Cremation was, therefore, as the arrangement of the cemetery suggested, practised contemporaneously with inhumation throughout the whole of the Pagan Saxon period; and the range of types found (v. p. 26) seems to show that it was practised as freely towards the close of the period as at the beginning.

CONCLUSIONS

The following conclusions may be drawn concerning the community for which the cemetery served, and its relation to the other communities of the neighbourhood.

The settlement was a typical Anglian one; the characteristic objects of this culture—cruciform fibulae, small-long fibulae, wrist-clasps, girdle-hangers and square-headed fibulae—are all represented, the first three in abundance. Cremation is predominant.

The community evidently settled very early; the presence of

women and children at an early date and the uniformity in the type of grave-goods show that the people were from the first true settlers, not merely raiders.

The settlement was evidently a peaceful one, and apparently the community remained undisturbed throughout the period during which the cemetery was in use; very few weapons were found; there is a large proportion of elderly men; and it is not recorded that a single skeleton showed marks of violence.

Further, the grave-goods suggest that the settlement was to some extent isolated from peaceful intercourse as well as from hostile attack. Considering the size of the cemetery the objects are not very numerous and, on the whole, not elaborate nor apparently very valuable. There is very little variety, for instance, in the dress fastenings, fibulae, buckles, wrist-clasps, etc.; these, moreover, appear to become rarer as the period advances; there are scarcely any examples of the later developments. Again, there are no imported objects except some glass, evidently fragments of drinking vessels, which appears to be an import of late VI (v. Fox, p. 294).

This poverty and lack of development in VI is more striking if the cemetery be compared with two others that have much in common with it—that at Little Wilbraham (188 inhumation, 121 cremation interments) and at St John's College, Cambridge (30 inhumation, 100 cremation interments).

In both these cemeteries cremation is very common, as at Girton; both appear to have been in use for about the same length of time—the former from mid V all through VI, the latter from mid V till early VII (Fox, pp. 262, 243). There is a close similarity between many objects found in these cemeteries, both in general types (v. the plates in Neville's *Saxon Obsequies*) and in particular objects: e.g. a girdle-hanger with unusual ornament from Little Wilbraham (Fox, Pl. XXXIII, 5) and a fibula from St John's (Fox, Pl. XXVII, 1, cf. 2), one quoit fibula from St John's exactly resembles that figured on Pl. IV, 2 c. These places were evidently occupied by people very closely related to those at Girton. Both the cemeteries, however, show greater variety, especially in objects of VI date, than is found at Girton.

Again, the fact that cremation was practised so freely in this

PLATE X

SCULPTURED STONE, FROM RUBBISH-PIT

cemetery till a very late date seems to show that the community was for some reason or other not so accessible to new influences from without as the others of the district; it is usual to find that cremation died out gradually as the Pagan period advanced; whereas here it seems no less flourishing and perhaps even more popular at the last than at the first.

These peculiarities of the cemetery lead one to consider its position and that of the settlement to which it belonged. The site of the latter can only be surmised. The nearest water—the first essential for a settlement—is the Washpit Brook, which runs through the westernmost part of the village of Girton, and flows into a tributary of the Ouse. Map V in Fox's *Archaeology of Camb. Region* shows that this area (the village of Girton) was "more or less clear of forest" in prehistoric times. The village was in existence at the time of the Domesday survey; it is natural to conjecture therefore that this was the site of the Pagan village also.

One might at first suppose that this district would be colonised by settlers coming along the Old West Water rather than up the Cam; but Fox's map shows that there is no evidence for any other Pagan Saxon settlement either along that tributary on the southern margin of the Fens in this area, or along that part of the Ouse into which it flows. The Girton settlement obviously belonged, as the grave-goods indicate, to the Cam valley group, and was the furthest NW of these; it stood on the edge of an area partly fen, partly "densely forested," extending for miles on three sides, so that the only open approach was from the SE along the Roman road.

It is probable, therefore, that one section of the group of settlers who entered the district by the Cam, instead of continuing up the river, or settling near it, turned off at Cambridge and went up the Roman Cambridge-Godmanchester road, and made a settlement in the first practicable place they reached— a spot made more attractive, perhaps, by having been cultivated during the Roman period.

The occurrence of a Bronze Age burial (*v.* p. 32) is of interest, showing that the site was attractive to settlers at a period very remote from that which we have been discussing.

A. EVIDENCE FOR THE OCCUPATION OF THE SITE IN THE
BRONZE AGE AND IN THE ROMAN PERIOD

1. **Bronze Age.** A fragment of pottery of this period was found on the Girton site and is preserved in the Cambridge Museum. It is of coarse, thick ware, roughly incised with diagonal lines, and is evidently part of the rim of a cinerary urn of overhanging rim type, similar to that from Soham figured by Fox on Pl. III, belonging to the 15 C. B.C. This suggests that the site may have been in use as a burial ground as far back as the Middle Bronze Age.

2. **Roman Period.** Two Roman cremation burials, and what may be traces of a third, were discovered by Jenkinson, who gave the following account of their position: "They were in a line running WNW and ESE, or approximately parallel to the direction of the Roman road. The Roman remains consisted principally of the contents of 2 square wooden boxes, the form of which was clearly traced by the nails and the pieces of wood adhering to them" (*C.A.S. Rep.* XLI). The third burial evidently lay in a line with these, as Jenkinson's notes state that "somewhere near Grave 40 the workmen hashed up a large portion of a Roman earthenware bottle, white with daubs of orange-red; paste in fracture brick-red. This is suggestive of a possibly Roman burial anciently disturbed."

The table on p. 33 shows the contents of the first two graves.

*Discussion of Objects*

(1) **Glass.** The cinerary urns are of thick green glass, each having a reeded handle. The hexagonal urn has a raised pattern of circles and semicircles on the external base. The small cylindrical vessels are of colourless glass, and are very fine and delicate.

The dish is light green glass; its decoration is very unusual; it consists of a bird-form, probably a duck, incised in outline on the external base, within the circle formed by the foot-ring. Incised decoration on glass is very rare in Roman Britain—

PLATE XI

CONTENTS OF ROMAN CREMATION GRAVES

TABLE OF THE CONTENTS OF TWO ROMAN CREMATION
GRAVES (*v*. Pl. XI)

| Vessel used as cinerary urn | "Samian ware" | Other pottery | Glass | Miscellaneous |
|---|---|---|---|---|
| I (*v*. Pl. XI, 1). Square glass bottle 10 ins. high. | 2 Paterae; both Dragendorf 18/31. Potter's marks: (1) PAULLI. M. (2) MONTANUS. | 2 jugs, "unglazed cream-coloured ware." 1 dish of coarse cream ware. | Small cylindrical vessel (very fragmentary, and therefore not figured, but similar to that in Gr. II). | Iron lamp-stand and rod for suspension. Nails about 4 ins. long round edge of grave. "In one place were widely spread remains of iron, but only some rivets could be collected." |
| II (*v*. Pl. XI, 2). Hexagonal glass bottle 9 ins. high. | 2 Paterae; both Dragendorf 18/31. Potter's marks: (1) BORILLI. M. (2) PATER ATI. OF. 1 cup, Dragendorf form 33. Potter's mark: PAULI. F. | Jug 5·8 ins. high, of coarse cream ware. Glazed bowl with white striae about ¼ in. apart. | Small cylindrical vessel. "Decanter." "Unguentarium with the mark of C. Lucreti Festivi."* Glass dish. | Iron lamp-stand with rod for suspension. 8 metal (bronze) bosses and 8 metal rings, with numerous scraps of iron and bronze. |

\* Figured by C. C. Babington, *Ancient Cambridgeshire*, p. 39.

Ward, in his discussion of glass (*Roman Era in Britain*, p. 179), cites no example of it. Even more rare was the mark "C. Lucreti Festivi" stamped on the unguentarium, which has most unfortunately been lost. This was probably the maker's name; Ward (*Roman Era*, p. 182) mentions that some glass bottles, similar to those used here as cineraries, have initials on the base, but he cites no example of a full name. We can obtain no information about this unguentarium beyond Jenkinson's note quoted in the above table of grave-goods.

(2) **Pottery.**

(*a*) "*Samian*." Paullus and Borillus were potters of the Antonine period, and worked at Lezoux (Oswald and Price, *Terra Sigillata*, p. 62). Pateratus flourished during the period A.D. 140–180 (May, *Silchester*, p. 144). Montanus was a potter of East Gaul. These cremation burials may therefore be dated in the 2nd century.

(*b*) The pottery bowl in Gr. 11 is evidently an imitation of a glass vessel, such as that exhibited in Case 45 in the Cambridge Museum. This bowl has an olive-green glaze, representing the brownish glass of the latter vessel, and has white striae about ¼ in. apart, representing the fluting of the glass.

(3) **Metal Bosses**, etc. These were found lying in a circle and were evidently the fittings of a wooden casket. The bosses are moulded to represent boars' heads; they may be compared with a similar set of fittings from Welwyn exhibited in the Ransom case in the Camb. Mus., which are in the form of lions' heads. The rings were evidently fitted on with iron clamps.

### Inhumation burials

The Graves numbered 28 and 34 on the Plan may be either Saxon or Roman (*v.* p. 17). It seems on the whole more probable that they are Roman; the fact that they lie within a fairly short distance of the cremation graves in a line roughly parallel to the Roman road may afford some support to this view.

Small groups of burials such as those just described were common in Roman Britain near a dwelling-house (Ward, *Roman Era*, p. 137). No foundations of any building have been discovered on this site, but enough evidence of other sorts exists to prove that a Roman dwelling-house stood in the near neighbourhood.

### B. Evidence for the existence of a Dwelling-house on or near this Site

#### 1. Building Material

(1) *Stone.* A great quantity of stone, chiefly oolite, sometimes worked, sometimes in rough blocks, was found during the excavation of the Anglian cemetery. Many graves were bordered with such stones—e.g. Gr. 3 was "covered with a large mass of stones some of which seemed to have belonged to some building as they showed signs of rectangular form here and there, one cylindrical." Similar stone was sometimes used to cover an urn, e.g. that near Gr. 25. These stones were evidently scattered all over the site. Jenkinson notes, for instance, that "in one place within 10 yds. of the interments the ground was full of fragments of stone which seemed to bear no relation

PLATE XII

DESIGN ON GLASS DISH, ROMAN CREMATION GRAVE II

to the graves" (*C.A.S. Rep.* XLVI). Several pieces of oolite, again, were found 3 ft. NW of Gr. 7.

(2) *Bricks and Tiles.* In 2 graves—9 and 56—were found Roman bricks embedded in mortar, evidently used like the stone to form part of the border of the grave. Besides these, parts of a hypocaust tile and of 2 roofing tiles have been preserved at Girton but are unfortunately not mentioned in Jenkinson's notes, so that it is not known on what part of the site they were found.

## 2. *Pottery*

Fragments of pottery were evidently scattered about the site also. They were found in graves, e.g. Gr. 29, and loose in the earth, e.g. "North of Gr. 42 a trench was encountered 4½ ft. wide, with steep sides; the soil was mixed with much white clay and pieces of Roman pottery occurred." Some of these fragments are of "Samian ware," and many of pale grey ware, of the ordinary domestic type. One vessel of this ware, which has been restored, is in form characteristic of the second half of the 1st century.

## 3. *Rubbish Pit*

The following account from Jenkinson's notes may be quoted:

"Some 4 feet east of S (i.e. NE of Gr. 59) we struck into a black earth pit containing bones of domestic animals, some charcoal, a few oysters, and some 2 dozen fragments of Roman pottery. At 2 ft. 8 ins. occurred a Saxon urn with bones *in situ*. At 3 ft. 8 ins. a human skeleton with a bronze buckle and 1 blue glaze bead about the left shoulder (*sic*). Another lay on its left side, next to that a child. Two more children had been placed with their heads about at the centres of the bodies of their elders. The pit extended a few feet to NW, and 2 Roman vessels in fragments were found in one of the lowest strata, one mixed with animal bones. At the bottom of the pit occurred 5 large pieces of sculptured stone, one being a spirited representation of a lion's head" (*v.* Pls. IX and X).

These pieces of sculptured stone are among the most interesting finds in this cemetery. Besides the lion's head (Pl. IX) there are three fragments which evidently represent portions of the paws and tail. The fifth fragment represents a human torso

(Pl. X); this is about two-thirds life-size. Only the back is recognisable, the front having crumbled away. It is difficult to say from what structure these stones can have come. They might have formed either part of the architectural ornament of the dwelling-house or part of an elaborate tomb, such as occur by the Roman roads in Italy. We have sent photographs of them to Mr R. G. Collingwood, M.A., F.S.A., of Oxford, and asked his opinion; he has very kindly given us permission to quote the following extract from his reply. "There seems to me no doubt that the lion's head is Romano-British. These lions are very common; whether this was part of a sepulchral monument, or whether it was merely an architectural ornament, there seems to me no way of deciding....Clearly it is good work, nothing amateurish about it, and there is too little of it to say much about its style." Rubbish pits of this sort are, of course, common near Roman dwelling-houses, but it is not usual to find human skeletons in them. There is, moreover, no evidence to show whether the skeletons are those of Romanised Britons or of Anglo-Saxons.

The worked freestone, hypocaust and roofing tiles, the bricks and the rubbish pit prove that a Roman dwelling-house, presumably connected with the Roman graves, existed near the site. It is unsafe to draw conclusions from the presence of the single vessel of 1st century type, but it may be held to be certain that the house was in existence in the second half of the 2nd century; and the Castor ware beakers of 4th century type, whether the graves in which they were found are Roman or Anglo-Saxon, show that it was occupied till near the end of the Roman period. The position of the sculptured stones in the pit, however, and the presence of skeletons near the surface, present some difficulty. The sculptured stones probably formed part of an elaborate tomb, and their position at the bottom of the pit shows that the site was occupied after the destruction of whatever structure they belonged to, whether tombs or house. It is difficult to explain this, and equally difficult to account for the burial of two adults and three children in the rubbish pit. They seem to be of post-Roman date, but they were evidently not disposed with the care that is apparent in the normal Anglian burials in this cemetery.

# INDEX

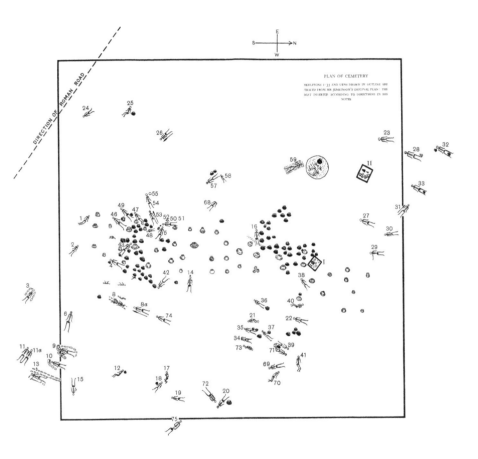

The material originally positioned here is too large for reproduction in this reissue. A PDF can be downloaded from the web address given on page iv of this book, by clicking on 'Resources Available'.